"By picking up this book, you have

in the process of putting an estate plan in place for your

family. Your family will thank you for this – they really will

(you just won't be here to hear them). Ravi is one of the

most passionate and experienced estate planners in the

businesses and his writing will be an essential resource

for anyone who is looking to begin their estate planning

journey."

Matthew Smith, Managing Director of
Buckingham Gate Wealth Management

"No one wants to talk about dying — period. But what

folks don't talk about enough is that personalized estate

planning is invaluable for securing your loved ones'

well-being and fulfilling your legacy. Knowing the intri-

cacies of estate law can ensure your plan reflects your

exact hopes and dreams, leaving nothing to chance.

For peace of mind today, and smooth sailing tomorrow,

experienced estate planning counsel is one of the wisest investments you can make.

What We Leave Behind is a comprehensive guide to estate planning from a seasoned estate planner with many years of experience helping clients protect their families and assets. Using realistic scenarios and compelling storytelling, Ravi explains how to structure your wealth so you can invest in your family's future.

Whether you're just getting started with a will or want to review and update your existing strategy, this book is a must-read to gain valuable peace of mind about your family's future and your hard-earned wealth."

Steve Gordon, Bestselling Author of The Million Dollar Book and Unstoppable Referrals

"A clear and concise guide to understanding this sensitive but vital subject. Ravi writes with a passion and commitment that I've come to know personally through our discussions about life, death, and the importance of understanding the needs of others. Ravi is more than just a talented professional in his field of expertise; he is a sensitive human being, deep thinker and problem solver."

David R Cotterill, Personal Development Coach & Three Principles Practitioner

---

"In all my dealings with Ravi, I have found that he has a unique ability to make complex matters accessible for clients. He achieves this by taking the time to look at each individual's circumstances rather than merely starting by presenting a readymade solution. Going forward, clients can see the value of their legacy that they can pass on for the benefit of the next generation."

Paul Reynolds, Tax Partner at Haslers

What We Leave Behind

ISBN: 9798387013874

Imprint: Independently published

Copyright 2023, Ravi Solanki

This book was produced in collaboration with
Write Business Results Limited. For more information on
their business book and marketing services, please visit
www.writebusinessresults.com or contact the team via
info@writebusinessresults.com.

This book does not constitute financial advice and the
reader should not regard any of the financial information
provided herein as a personal recommendation. The advice
and strategies contained herein may not be suitable for every
situation. It is your responsibility to seek the services of a
competent professional if professional assistance is required.
Neither the authors nor the publisher shall be liable for
damages arising herefrom.

Will writing, trusts and estate planning are not regulated by the
Financial Conduct Authority. This book has been designed to
provide a generic guide to estate planning and should not be
used as a substitute for taking professional advice. If you are
unsure, you should seek professional advice from an estate
planning expert.

What We Leave Behind

DISCOVER HOW TO LEAVE YOUR LEGACY AND PROTECT YOUR WEALTH

RAVI SOLANKI

Acknowledgements

To my brother Kamal Solanki for introducing me to the world of estate planning.

To my parents for providing support and challenging me to grow as a person every day.

To all of my coaches, mentors and advisors who have helped me to navigate the entrepreneur roller-coaster. In particular Phillip Burton, Doug Bennett, Lisa Slater, Theresia Venier, Steve Gordon, Matthew Smith, Philip Calvert and Barry Cohen. You've helped me see the potential in myself, and thank you for pointing me in the right direction with your guidance and wisdom.

To the following authors – Steve Gordon, Jim Rohn, Robert Kiyosaki, Ivan Misner, Dan Sullivan, Brad Sugars, Sydney Banks, Michael Neill - your books have been life changing.

My team at Sure Wealth and all of my colleagues who are instrumental in creating solutions for my clients.

To all of my wonderful clients – thank you for trusting me to ensure your legacy lives on.

Finally a big thanks to Georgia Kirke and Ivan Meakins for your patience and helping me bring this book to life.

Dedication

To those who want to leave a legacy behind…

this is for you.

Contents

Foreword

You probably were not aware when you woke up today that this book would be on your reading list. It is likely you are devoting time to it following the loss of some-one close, a loved one, family or friend. Perhaps you have reached an age where you would like to have your affairs in order and this is something else to tick off your list. More likely you are a person who purposefully needs to ensure you have control of your wishes and that whomever deals with your estate is well positioned to follow your desired plan.

Either way, the time spent with this book will put your mind in the right place. Ravi is a kind and gentle person whom, in the world of estate planning for both personal and business, has achieved the highest certification through his investment in study and practice ensuring his professional advice is sound and reliable.

His calm approach to understanding your needs and desired outcomes is achieved from years of understanding people in the City (London) and following a pathway that he truly believes in.

As you read you will find some parts touching – there are several family stories that you will relate to. I had a separate pen and paper to make notes. Ravi does ask some questions, all of which you have the answers to. As you turn the pages, there is no rush to complete the read – in fact, I believe to get the best from it you may need to cover the pages two or three times.

Ravi, in his genuine way, is raising awareness for what is inevitable for all of us. The question for me and my family was understanding the outcomes of not taking some future planning professional advice and most importantly acting on it.

Your time on the following pages will open your mind to investing time in planning for your future wishes to be met. In a time of inevitable uncertainty for others, make the pathway of passing less of a burden for those you elect to ensure your wishes are followed.

Ravi on behalf of my family, thank you.

Phillip Burton

Director, Father, Grandfather

What We Leave Behind

Introduction

Death is one of the few experiences that all of us share. As we go through life, all of us will lose people we care about, and eventually both you and I will pass as well. From an early age, we come to understand that we are all mortal, and yet it's very rare that we actually take time to talk about what death means for us – our hopes and fears, the memories we leave behind, and the dreams we have for our family after we're gone.

It's no surprise that death is a taboo topic, both in the media and our personal lives. It's scary, and painful. Who wants to spend their day thinking about the passing of their friends and family, or reflecting on their own mortality? Most of the time we do our best to avoid thinking of it, let alone talking about it. Sometimes this means that when the moment comes, we find we aren't emotionally prepared, making the experience of death much more difficult.

There's another side to death we also tend to ignore – the practical aspect. What will happen to my property when I die? Who will receive my wealth? How can I be sure my loved ones will be provided for? These questions can bring all sorts of complications – legal difficulties, family conflicts and tax bills. If they aren't properly handled, they can make the emotional side of death even harder to cope with.

As a professional estate planner, people come to me to take the stress out of the practical side of death. I do this by helping them decide their priorities, make plans and manage the transfer of their assets to the next generation. Along with my colleagues at Sure Wealth, I take care of the legal technicalities so that my clients can look forward to the rest of their lives with peace of mind.

But that's not all. For me, it's not enough just to reduce your anxiety. I want to change how you think about death. My goal – and the goal of this book – is to help you approach your own passing with a positive attitude.

Instead of worrying about what might go wrong after you're gone, I want you to start envisioning the kind of legacy you want to leave, and the benefits it'll provide for your family. Once you do this, death becomes another of life's challenges – one to be faced head on, not shied away from.

By picking up this book, you've shown you're ready to take on this challenge. Throughout the following chapters, you'll find everything you need to start planning the future of your family. Let's be clear though – this isn't a do-it-yourself guide. Estate planning requires years of training and professional expertise. The point of this book is to give you an insight into the power of estate planning and to help you find the right estate planner achieve your legacy goals.

The book is divided into two halves. The first half of the book – Chapters 1 to 4 – is all about you. It will help you sketch a picture of your existing wealth, and start making a plan for how you can use it to support your family for decades to come. Even more importantly, it will guide you in finding your own answers to the really big questions – What is my vision for the future of my family? What lessons, memories and values do I want to leave behind? These answers will be the foundation on which your estate plan is built.

In the second half – Chapters 5 to 8 – you'll find practical advice and insights drawn from my years of experience in the business. These will help you understand the basics of estate planning, so that you can have an informed conversation with a professional when the time is right. They'll also show you what you should look for in a good estate planner.

By the end of this book, you will have achieved the following:

- Built a picture of your existing wealth, and started to think about your plan for how to pass it on.
- Understood the risks involved with passing on your wealth, and how estate planning can mitigate them.
- Formed an image of your ideal estate planner and what you want from your relationship with them.

Before we get to all that though, it's essential to make sure that we're approaching these issues with the right mindset. This means being able to face up to the fact of your own mortality, and to confront it as a challenge and an opportunity. This might sound a little daunting at first, but don't worry – the next chapter will tell you all you need to know about the benefits of being Death Positive.

What We Leave Behind

Chapter 1

Understanding Our Own Mortality

"Death is the destination we all share. No one has ever
escaped it. And that is as it should be, because death is very
likely the single best invention of life. It is life's change
agent. It clears out the old to make way for the new."

-- Steve Jobs

A Good Death

If you ask 100 people, "What does it mean to lead a
good life?", you'll probably get 100 different replies. For
some, living well means travelling the globe and seek-
ing out new experiences; for others, it's about making
a difference, and knowing that they've left the world a
better place than they found it. Everyone has their own
unique answer, because we all know what a good life
means to us.

But what about a good death? I bet most of us are not so sure. Perhaps we've never even thought about it. This is strange, because the moment of a person's death is the time when we reflect on their achievements and their failures, the lives they've touched and the memories they leave behind. It's only when a person has died that we can define how they lived. A good life and a good death are two sides of the same coin.

Imagine a person – let's call him Robert – who's lived their life in the fullest way possible, whatever that means for you. Perhaps he has experienced professional success, donated money to charity, raised a happy and loving family – or even all three! He's worked hard and been well-rewarded for it, but he isn't interested in wealth for its own sake. He uses his money to enhance the lives of others, whether by giving thoughtful gifts, helping his loved ones achieve their ambitions or supporting worthy causes.

Robert's one weakness is that he is so determined to squeeze the most from every second of every day that he absolutely refuses to discuss, or even think about, what will happen after he's gone. As he gets older, his loved ones sometimes ask if he's thought about settling his affairs. He laughs them off – why waste time stressing about the future when the present has so much to offer? Robert goes on living every day as if it's his last, while his friends and family are left to worry what comes next.

When Robert finally does pass on at the end of a long and happy life, he leaves his family a complicated legacy. On the one hand there are words of wisdom and fond memories; on the other, a mountain of legal mess. Since he left no instructions for how he wanted his wealth to be shared, his loved ones are forced to spend months, or even years, negotiating and bargaining. They still look back on him with fondness, but this positive emotion is now mixed with regret.

Robert might be a figment of our imaginations, but I'm sure we all know someone like him in our real lives. Perhaps we even recognise a bit of him in ourselves. Nobody likes to dwell on thoughts of their own mortality. But as Robert's story shows, even the most well-lived life will be left unfulfilled if we fail to plan for the grand finale. We should all aspire to die as we have lived, in line with our values and with care and consideration for those we loved the most.

The purpose of this book is to guide you through the process of planning your personal legacy. It contains practical advice and step-by-step guides drawn from my years of experience in the estate planning business. But before we get to that, let's acknowledge one thing: **Death is a difficult subject to talk about.**

We have to take this difficulty seriously. It can't be glossed over, because if we can't face up to the fact that one day we all have to die, then planning for what happens when that day finally comes is extremely difficult!

So, in this first chapter I want to share with you some of what I've learned about how to approach this sensitive topic.

The Death Taboo

Death is a fact of life, but in our modern society many of us are unprepared to face it, both spiritually and practically. We aren't taught about it at school, and our loved ones prefer not to talk about it until we have no choice. This is understandable. We don't like to think about the uncertainty and loss which could potentially befall us at any moment. By sticking our heads in the sand, we feel like we achieve security.

But just because we've shut our eyes to the problem doesn't mean it's gone away. In fact, by blinding ourselves to reality, we make things far worse. Death is always a tragedy, but by failing to prepare for the inevitable we risk turning it into a crisis. This can be avoided, but only if we overcome the taboo that prevents us from seeing death as a part of everyday life.

Media narratives have a big part to play here. In news coverage and in TV and film, death is either sensational-ised (think of how many serial killers you've seen on your telly over the last 20 years) or grim and depressing. This makes us feel powerless and lost. Death is presented as something that is done to us, a force completely beyond our control. In this case, what else is there to do except ignore it?

Of course, death can be an upsetting experience. But is that all it is? If we stop and reflect for a moment on our own lives, we'll soon see that there are all kinds of differ-ent emotions that can be associated with mortality. Take a moment and think about the passing of someone you really admired or cared for. What do you feel? Sadness and loss, sure, but I bet there are other feelings mixed in there as well. Pride. Respect. Gratitude.

This is one of those cases where we need to pay less attention to the media, and more to our own experience. The lesson of our own lives teaches us that death is complex. It can be painful. It can be bittersweet. It can be life-affirming. In fact, there are as many different ways of facing death as there are people in the world. Once we've realised this, we no longer need to feel so powerless. We have choices.

If there's one idea I'd like you to take away from this book, it's that death can be seen as a source of possibilities. By taking the initiative, by proactively planning for what will happen after we're gone, we can give ourselves the power to decide what kind of death we will have. We can choose how our passing impacts our loved ones, and in what way we will be remembered.

Granted, learning to see death as a source of possibility isn't an easy task. How do we achieve this shift in mindset? For me, it was a process of education, based partly on my own personal experience, and partly on learning how other cultures have dealt with death at different moments in human history.

Death in different cultures and traditions

My first personal experience of death was in 1999, just a few days before the new millennium. An uncle of mine had passed. In my family's culture, it's traditional to bring the body home and say prayers over the open casket. As my relatives gathered around to pay their respects, I felt sadness and loss, but also curiosity.

My parents told me that my uncle had entered a long sleep from which he would never wake. They meant to comfort me, because when we sleep we are at peace, and nothing can hurt us. At the time I was reassured, but on a deeper level the idea left me dissatisfied. I needed to know more. What does a person leave behind them when they die? How do their actions go on shaping the world even after they're gone? What can we do to keep their memory alive?

In the years to come, both of my grandmothers' – who I was always very close to – also passed away. I was heartbroken of course, but also deeply thankful for all the happy memories and gifts of advice and wisdom they'd shared with me while I knew them. Their bodies were gone, but I knew they would live on in the hearts and minds of myself and my family.

As I grew older, these early experiences of loss drove me to find out more about the stories that different cultures have used to make sense of death down the years.

The more I learned, the more I understood that our modern western culture is very unusual. First, because death is generally not talked about except at very particular moments – at funerals, memorials and so on. In other cultures throughout history, it is far more common for death to be discussed as part of everyday life – as something to be guarded against, to be prepared for, even celebrated.

Second, because we tend to see death as something final, as an ending. In other cultures, death is more likely to be understood as a change. For example, in classical Greek and Roman mythologies, the underworld was a place you could travel to, and both gods and mortals made journeys between the realms of the living and the dead.

In burial traditions all across the ancient world, people were interred with their possessions, and sometimes even their pets! Egyptian pharaohs were entombed in gold sarcophaguses, surrounded by their treasures. Viking warlords were laid to rest in a longship filled with weapons and plunder, which was then set on fire and pushed out to sea. Death was seen as a voyage, and it was important that the traveller was properly equipped.

The various religions and faiths of this world all have different beliefs and attitudes towards death and the afterlife, but when we place them all side-by-side they show us that throughout history, human beings have always prepared themselves for death with the utmost care. This is because it was always understood that a person's story does not end when their heart stops beating. It continues through their achievements, the lives they touched and the wealth and wisdom they pass on to their descendants.

This is a lesson that today's social media-influenced culture, with its emphasis on instant gratification, has tended to forget. There's nothing wrong with living in the moment, so long as we remember that at the same time, every choice we make is a contribution to our legacy.

I want you to take a moment, and really think about the idea of legacy. What does it mean to you? Take your time – your answer may be more important than you realise!

Defining your legacy

What do I mean by the word "legacy"? It's quite simple – "legacy" defines all the ways in which a person continues to shape the world even after they've passed away. This goes from the smallest, most personal gestures – think of your memories of being given sweets by your grandparents on a childhood holiday – to the most towering global achievements.

Take the example of Steve Jobs, the founder of Apple, who lost his life to cancer in 2011 at the age of 56. Jobs has been gone from the world for 12 years, but the company he built has touched the lives of millions. His ideas continue to influence the design of new products, meaning that Steve Jobs' vision is still defining our shared future, even though he's no longer with us.

We can't all be Steve Jobs, but all of us leave a legacy, whether we're conscious of it or not. And in fact, this is the most important choice that we all face. We can go on living our lives without thinking about what we want to pass on to the next generation, or we can take responsibility for creating a legacy that will last for years after we're gone. We can leave a financial and legal mess for our descendants to clean up, or we can give them a gift which represents not just our material wealth, but all the wisdom we've built up over a lifetime.

This book will guide you through the process of planning your legacy. For some of us, this might be something we enjoy, an opportunity to reflect on a lifetime of hard-earned accomplishments. For others, it may be more of a challenge. It could involve tough choices, or difficult conversations with friends and loved ones.

If you're one of those people who finds this topic hard to confront, don't worry – you're not alone. And in fact, you've already taken the first, and in many ways hardest, step towards taking control of your legacy. When you opened this book, you sent yourself a message:

"I understand that one day I'll be gone, while my loved ones will go on without me."

From this initial awareness we can build towards acceptance. Once acceptance is achieved, then planning can begin.

What is the importance of planning?

Planning is the key to taking control of your legacy. Without a plan, you'll always be reacting, trying to catch up to events as they happen. Plan well, and you will be ready to respond calmly and confidently to any eventuality. Later in this book, I'll guide you step-by-step through the process of planning your legacy. First, however, we need to understand what planning really means.

When we talk about having a plan, the first thing we think of is probably a kind of checklist, with tasks waiting to be ticked off. For sure, lists are a useful tool in the planning process, but they are far from the most important part. A list is just a piece of paper. It can be put away in a drawer and forgotten about. Or perhaps circumstances change, and now parts of the list are irrelevant. You'll have to tear it up and start again.

For this reason, I like to stress that planning is not just an activity, but a state of mind. It begins by deciding what kind of future you want to see for your loved ones, and which values you want to pass on to the next generation. This is the heart of your plan, everything else you do flows from it.

There's a famous quote by the heavyweight boxer Mike Tyson: "Everyone has a plan, until they get punched in the mouth." Life has an unfortunate tendency to punch all of us in the mouth every now and again. It's in moments like this that we find out what our plans are really worth. If your plan is truly based on your vision and your values, it will survive everything life has to throw at you.

Being death positive

In my time in this business, I've known people who spent years procrastinating over putting their affairs in order. The longer they left it, the more the stress built up, and the more difficult it became for them to engage with the problem. In a couple of cases, I've seen people pass away before they've finished putting their plans in place. In these tragic circumstances, one person's procrastination leads to a whole host of unpleasant complications for their family.

As a professional, cases like these help remind me how vital the work of an estate planner can be. Good planning releases us from anxiety and procrastination. Instead of dwelling on our fears, we confront them. By getting all the issues out in the open, documenting them and agreeing a way forward, we break down the problems until they are manageable. I can't promise to take the sadness out of death, but by working together we can find a way to deal with it on your terms.

But estate planning isn't just about reducing negative emotions. By taking control of your legacy, you also generate new opportunities to go on shaping the world even after you've left it for good. This reflects an attitude I like to call "Death Positive" – a mindset which sees mortality as a challenge and an opportunity to be embraced with all our hearts.

Being Death Positive means taking the time to reflect on the big questions. What really matters to me? How will I be remembered? How can I pass on my experiences and values to the next generation? How can I leave a legacy that will be of value to the children of my children, and those who come after them? It means seeing the moment of our passing as our last great opportunity to leave a lasting mark on the world.

Certainty in an uncertain world

The last 3 years has seen the whole world live through a time of great uncertainty, fear and stress. The Covid-19 pandemic has brought all of us face-to-face with death in an entirely new way. Meanwhile, climate change has forced us to contemplate the death of the planet itself. Events like these can make planning for the future feel like an even more daunting task. But we have a choice as to how we respond.

Over the past few years I've noticed an interesting pattern. Increasingly, we're seeing clients in their 20s and 30s getting in touch to explore the process of planning their legacy. Some might see this as a depressing sign, but to me, this is a great source of hope. Young people are responding to our current climate of uncertainty not by putting their heads in the sand, but by proactively taking responsibility for the future.

This is a perfect example of what I mean by being Death Positive. Instead of being overwhelmed by uncertainty, young people are responding by taking control. I think we should applaud this behaviour, and try to learn from their example. If we do, it could be that we are on the verge of a shift away from our current "microwave culture" of instant gratification, and towards one based more on showing more responsibility for our shared future.

Over the course of the rest of this book, I'm going to walk you through all the steps you'll need to take to ensure your wealth brings the greatest possible benefit to your descendants. Later on, we'll get into the practical stuff – planning, risk, tax and so on. Right now though, we need to answer a deeper question. What kind of legacy do you want to leave for future generations?

Chapter 2

Leaving a Legacy

"The greatest use of life is to spend it for
something that will outlast it."

--William James

How do you want to be remembered?

If you died tomorrow, what would you want people to
say about you? How would you want them to feel when
they thought of you? Would you want to be remembered
for your professional achievements? Your kindness and
generosity? For the way you took care of your family?

One thing's for sure – we'll all be remembered for something. Whether we intend it or not, we all leave a mark on
the world and on the lives of other people. The choice
for us is to decide whether we want to take responsibility

for the impression we leave behind. The way that people will speak and feel about us once we've passed away depends on the decisions we make right now.

There are two ways we can shape the mark we leave on the world. The first is through the way we live our lives day in and day out. Strong principles, good deeds and small acts of kindness all mount up to form the image people will keep with them after we're gone. If we make sure to behave with dignity and integrity while we're breathing, there's a decent chance that's how we'll be remembered once we're not.

The second is by making sure that when we go, we leave behind things that show people how we want to be remembered. In the past, kings and emperors built great monuments so that future generations would know of their strength and wisdom. That might be a bit flash for our tastes, but that doesn't mean that we can't also create structures that will remind our descendants what sort of person we were, and what mattered most to us. This is what it means to leave a legacy.

Your legacy can take many different forms. It could be an object, like some jewellery, or a piece of property, like a family home. It could be a video or a letter, in which you pass on your most precious memories and important lessons to your descendants. It could be a donation to a charitable foundation, or a trust fund that supports your children and their children for decades to come. It could be a combination of all of these things!

Estate planning can be a complicated business, with lots of moving parts, but at the end of the day it all comes back to this one basic question: What kind of legacy do you want to leave for your descendants? If you can't find the answer to this, then no amount of tax planning or will writing will help you. The point of this chapter, therefore, is to understand what legacy means to you. This is the foundation on which you build the rest of your plan.

What makes a legacy?

Legacies are made up of two elements – tangible and intangible assets. Tangible assets are material things like money, property, stocks and shares, personal documents and any other material items you or your family might value. They are important either because they are a source of wealth which can be used to secure your family's future, or because they have a special sentimental significance.

Intangible assets are a bit more complicated. At the end of the day, a human being is nothing more than a collection of experiences, lessons, stories and memories built up over the course of a lifetime. When we're young, we receive the experiences and lessons that our grandparents and parents pass down to us, and then as we grow we add to them with our own. As we become older, we have the chance to hand our stories on to the next generation.

These are our intangible assets. These stories and memories are containers for our emotions, our wisdom, and the hard-earned lessons we've learned over the course of our life. Some of them take the form of practical advice – how to sew on a button, or to cook a perfect Sunday roast (or curry!). Some of them are more like moral principles – the importance of good manners, or of doing the right thing even when it costs you.

Think about the lessons you learned from your parents and grandparents. They helped make you the person you are today – but that's not all. They also made your life easier. Getting advice from our elders is like being told a shortcut. Thanks to the tough times they put up with or the wrong turns they made, our journey was that much easier. Lessons that they had to learn the hard way are passed on to you in a few well-chosen words. This is their legacy.

The museum of your life

The secret of good estate planning is to bring the tangible and intangible parts of your legacy together. The material wealth you leave to your children should tell the stories you want them to remember you by.

Don't just think of your possessions as objects – they're exhibits in the museum of your life. Just as we go to a public museum to learn the history of our culture and society, so should your descendants be able to learn the history of their family – its traditions and values – from the things you leave behind. By taking time to plan how you distribute your wealth, you can make sure that it keeps these meanings for years to come.

Similarly, the way you pass down your wealth can be just as important as who gets what and how much. Rather than just leaving a lump sum, you can write a letter of wishes that will offer guidance to your family for how the money should be used or what causes it should be dedicated to. This way, you aren't just leaving them hard cash, but a reminder of your care and wisdom. We'll explore how you can do this later in the book.

We all have certain traditions that we follow in our lives. Some of these are specific to our family or our local community, others are shared with millions all over the world. We often take these traditions for granted. For instance, just because so many people celebrate Christmas on the 25 December every year, we might feel like this is the way things have always been and will always be in future.

But this isn't the case. Traditions are bigger than any individual, but they only survive because people choose to nourish them, passing them on from generation to generation. Your family is no different. If you and your loved ones have traditions or values that you think are worth preserving, then you have to make the conscious choice to make them a part of your legacy.

Why do legacies matter?

So far I've spoken in general terms about the importance of legacy. But in practice, legacy means different
things to different people. We'll all have our own motivations to plan for the future, and our own stories we want
to pass on. To help you think about what kind of legacy
you want to leave, it'll be helpful to explore some of the
different reasons people might have for wanting to leave
their mark on the world.

For some, leaving a legacy is a chance to enjoy their
success – the things they've achieved, the wealth
they've created. As parents, they've provided for their
family; as business owners or professionals, they've
delivered value for other people. When you take the time
to think about it, you'll find that you've touched the lives
of others in ways you didn't even realise. We all deserve
the opportunity to celebrate our contribution.

Others want to be sure that they've left their family, or
the world at large, in a better place than they found

them. Reflecting on a lifetime of hard work and good deeds can help show the impact they've had on the people around them.

It also allows them to make sure that their wealth continues to be used to support the causes that matter most to them. Donating to charity, supporting medical research, funding a university lectureship – these are all ways we can ensure that our values are passed onto future generations.

Perhaps the security of your family is your number one concern. I've met many clients who were keeping themselves awake at night worrying over what might happen to their children if something should happen to them. In other cases, it's the other way around, and it's the kids who are stressed because their parents don't have their affairs in order. Sometimes this can lead to tension in the family, or even full-on arguments.

The only way to address these fears is to face them head on. By setting out your legacy, you're not only taking care of what happens in the distant future, you're also creating peace of mind for your loved ones right now. Think of how much happier and more harmonious your family dinners will be once the subject of inheritance is off the table!

For some clients, their business is central to their legacy planning. This means having a plan for what happens to your company after you die – who gets your shares? Who takes on your responsibilities? How will succession be managed?

At the same time, it's also about making sure that your ethos lives on in the company you've created. Just as Coca Cola has guarded its secret recipe for more than 100 years, you should also make sure that the values and practices you've built into your business continue to define it for decades to come.

As you can see, there are as many motivations for building a legacy as there are people in the world! To help us understand how a client's motivations feed into their legacy planning, let's take a quick look at a case study drawn from my own experience as an estate planner.

Case Study: Raj and Pooja

Raj and Pooja are a married couple in their 50s with two adult children. Their daughter is, to her parents' great pride, happily married and financially independent. Their son, whose first marriage ended in divorce, has recently proposed to his new girlfriend, who Raj and Pooja are less than fond of. They are firm believers in the importance of family, and their priority is to ensure that their wealth is used to secure the future of their grandchildren.

Raj and Pooja's main motivations are:

• To minimise unnecessary tax on their estate.
• To make sure that each of them are properly supported in the event of the other's untimely death.
• To maximise the amount of wealth they leave to their descendants.

To support their goals, Sure Wealth created an advanced estate plan specially tailored to address their concerns. Its main provisions included:

1. In the event of either Raj or Pooja's death, the surviving partner would be able to benefit from all of the deceased's assets, but with certain protections to guarantee the future inheritance of their children.

2. If the surviving partner were to later remarry, their assets would be guaranteed to go to their children, rather than the new spouse.

3. When both Raj and Pooja pass away, their wealth will be kept in a trust, helping to minimise inheritance tax and ensuring their children use it in line with their wishes.

4. For their daughter, who is already financially independent, her inheritance will be kept separate from her family wealth, minimising her tax bills on her

current wealth and the legacy she will later pass on to her own children.

5. For their son, the bulk of his inheritance will be ring-fenced to protect it if he ever were to divorce again and ensure his children will see the benefits.

The lesson of all this is simple – as important as wealth and money are, that's not where you should start planning your legacy. Look first at your values, at the memories and stories you want to leave behind. Figure out what's driving you, and then let your wealth be the vehicle that gets you there.

Building your legacy

When you build your legacy, you're creating structures that are designed to outlive you by many years. Ideally, they will not only shape the lives of your children and grandchildren, but also those who come after them

– people who you will never meet and who will only know your memory second-hand.

Most of us probably aren't used to thinking this far into the future, but when planning our legacy we need to be thinking on a timeline of decades. What will the world look like in 30, 40, 50 years, and how can you continue supporting your family through the challenges and uncertainty to come?

When an architect designs a building, they are planning a structure that – if they've done their job well – will still be standing decades or even centuries after their death. Every part of their plan looks to the long term. When you're trying to envision your legacy, it can help to adopt an architect's mindset. What kind of shape will your legacy be in 100 years into the future?

Imagine your legacy as a building. The first thing it needs are strong foundations. These are your motivations, values and goals. You have to start with a clear idea of what you want your legacy to say about you as a person, and what stories you want it to tell to the next generation. Everything else rests on that.

Next you need a solid internal structure – the pillars, beams and load-bearing walls which keep the building upright. These are the legal documents and arrangements that are needed to ensure that your wishes are properly carried out, including wills, trusts, business succession plans and tax plans. This book will talk you through some of these things, but you'll need a qualified professional to make sure everything's in place.

Like most buildings, this one will be made up of different rooms, each representing a distinct part of your legacy. Each room can be filled with objects, memories, experiences – all your tangible and intangible assets. Thinking like this can help you break your legacy down, so you can see which parts go together, who gets what, and how much.

Some rooms will be open to many people. If you give money to charity or to an educational institution, they might even admit members of the public. Some will be tightly secured, like a safe or a vault, and only a few people will have access. Other rooms will be quiet spaces, for people to take a moment and remember what you meant to them.

These rooms will be connected by doors, hallways and stairs, designed to guide people around the house. These are the instructions, lessons and wisdom that you've left behind. They tell people when it's time to visit the different rooms, and for what reason. Some parts of the building will only be open when your beneficiary has reached a certain age or passed a personal milestone, such as getting a job or becoming a homeowner.

Allocate some time to plan your legacy. Share it with your family, see what they make of it. When the time comes to find an estate planner, you should show it to them as well. They can help you develop it – knock through this wall here, build an extension there. Just like home improvement, you'll find that you can probably handle putting up some shelves on your own, but for the serious stuff you'll need to call in the professionals.

Once you've got a clear idea of what you want from your legacy, you're ready to move on to your plan. This is the series of step-by-step actions that will help you put your vision for your family's future into practice.

Chapter 3

The Importance of Having a Life Plan

"If you don't know where you are going,
you'll end up someplace else."

--Yogi Berra

Hope for the best, prepare for the worst

We spoke in the last chapter about the importance of your legacy – the wealth, wisdom and values you leave to future generations. The key to taking control of your legacy is having a life plan. A well-made life plan can bring all sorts of benefits, and we'll discuss them soon. But to really understand the importance of planning, we need to know what can go wrong if we don't prepare for the inevitable.

What I'm about to describe is a worst-case scenario, but that doesn't mean it couldn't happen to you! In fact, it's scary how many people fail to take even the most basic steps to protect themselves from these risks.

If you don't make any plans for what happens to your wealth and assets after you die, then the government plan kicks in. This means that the law will decide who gets what. You and your family will have no control, and your property may not go to the people who really need or deserve it. Here are some of the main issues your family could face:

If you're unmarried and living with a partner, then they might not get anything. Your money will go instead to other members of your family.

If you're married with children, your wealth will be divided between your spouse and children, no matter what other agreements you might have had. This could mean kids under the age of 18 receiving assets they're too young to handle responsibly.

If you leave behind young children without naming a guardian, then social services will step in to decide who raises them.

If you leave no instructions for your inheritors, you give up the chance to decide how your wealth will be used. The three most common uses for inheritance are paying off debts, making a big purchase like a car, and going on holiday. Maybe that's fine – but wouldn't you like some say over how your money is spent?

If you don't decide who gets what, your death could set off a family dispute, with people arguing over what they think they were promised. Maybe you gave one child a gift during your lifetime, with the expectation that their brother or sister would get something extra when you're gone? If these promises aren't properly documented, it could lead to one child getting a double inheritance - the first during your lifetime, the second when you die. Is this fair on the other siblings?

If you don't have a plan, you cause stress both for yourself, as you worry over what might happen after you're gone, and your family, who are left to clear up the mess that you've left behind. Finding all the relevant documents, passwords, bank account numbers, house deeds and so on is not a job that should be left for your grieving spouse, partner or children.

If you haven't left clear directions for how your wealth is to be used then charities, public institutions and other causes that matter to you could miss out on a share of your legacy.

If you don't act now, you miss the opportunity to create tax-efficient structures that will protect your wealth for future generations.

To cut a long story short, if you don't make a proper life plan, then you'll be subjecting your family to a long, chaotic and stressful legal process. And at the end of the day, someone else gets to decide their future for them. Is that what you want for your legacy?

What's stopping you?

Nobody would wish any of this for themselves or their family. In fact, you'd think we'd all do everything we could to avoid it. But we don't. We stick our heads in the sand. We dither. We procrastinate. Why?

In my years in the estate planning business I've heard every excuse under the sun. Here are some of the main ones:

- Superstition – "I don't want to talk about death, I don't want to jinx it."
- Denial – "If I don't think about it, it'll never happen."
- Bravado – "I don't care, it doesn't matter to me what happens when I'm gone."
- Family tension – "I'm afraid to have difficult conversations with my kids and/or partner."
- Irresponsibility – "It's my husband/wife that handles all the finances."
- Lack of knowledge – "What should I do? Who can help me?"

Do you recognise any of these barriers in yourself? Let's be honest, we wouldn't be human if we didn't feel emotions like these every now and again. But when they're stopping us from doing what needs to be done, it's our responsibility to shake them off.

I want you to take a second now, and imagine yourself at the very end of your life. You're surrounded by your loved ones, both friends and family – all the people you'd want to be there to hear your last words. What are your thoughts at that moment? Are you filled with pride and contentment, ready to go to your final rest safe in the knowledge that everyone will be taken care of? Have you enjoyed the ride of life?

Are you free to focus on what really matters in those last few seconds – sharing your love and gratitude with the people who have been by your side through thick and thin? Or, are you filled with worry and regret over what happens next? Perhaps there's even a hint of shame at the mess you've left behind. Will you leave this planet with peace of mind, or with a feeling of sadness and guilt? Or did you wish you had worked harder for yourself and your family?

This might seem like a bleak picture, but the good news is that we get to decide which of these futures come true. We only have to snap out of our procrastination and take control. If you find yourself hesitating over whether it's time to start making your life plan, I want you to think back to the scene you've just pictured, and remember that your actions today will shape how it plays out.

Positive planning: Time to set your satnav

When you make your life plan, you're saving yourself and your family a world of stress and pain. But let's not just think about planning in terms of preventing negative outcomes. There are a whole host of benefits, many of which you've probably never thought of before.

Making a life plan is like setting your satnav. You start by choosing your destination. For you, this means deciding how you want things to look for you and your family when you reach the end of your life. What is your ideal outcome? Once you've answered this question, you can start setting out the steps you need to take to get there, just as picking a destination will allow your satnav to show you the best route.

Now things are a bit clearer. You can be confident that if you follow the right route, you'll get to your destination on time. But the benefit of a satnav isn't just that it gets you where you want to go. It's the peace of mind it provides while you're still on the journey. When you're guided by your satnav, you can afford to relax. Enjoy the ride. Admire the scenery.

It's the same with your plan. Once you know that everything will be sorted after you're gone, you'll feel so much freer to enjoy the rest of your life. What are your dreams for the next ten years? How do you want to spend your retirement? With your legacy taken care of, you'll know exactly how much you'll need to fulfil your other ambitions.

Another good thing about a satnav is that even if you decide that you need to change course, the computer will automatically find you a new route to your destination. As long as you still know where you want to go, it'll get you there. Likewise, once you've made your life plan, it's easy to amend or update it whenever you need to.

The planning process

We all know the importance of money. If your life plan is a satnav, money is like fuel. Your car won't get far without it. At the simplest level, planning is about organising your wealth and assets so they can help you arrive at your destination. But as we've already seen, it's also a more holistic process. It's about family, memory and pride. It's about making sure that your legacy reflects all the experiences and achievements you built up during your time on this planet. That's why I call it a "life plan".

In the previous chapter we discussed how your legacy can be divided into two parts – tangible and intangible assets. Tangible assets are things like money, property, stocks and shares, personal documents and any other material items you or your family might value. Intangible assets are the wisdom, memories and values you want to pass on to your descendants.

Your life plan is about combining these two halves to make a whole. If you get it right, then the way that you've chosen to organise your tangible assets (your wealth and property) will express the intangible assets (wisdom, memories, values) that you want your friends and family to carry with them into the future. Your decisions about what happens to your money and possessions will help people remember the lessons you wanted to pass on and the causes you stood for.

Life planning is a four-step process:

Step One: Defining your vision

Step Two: Where are you today?

Step Three: What are your risks?

Step Four: What are your solutions?

Let's break these steps down in more detail.

Step One: Defining your vision

Step One is about setting your satnav. You're deciding your final destination, both so you know where you want to get to and so you can make sure that the journey there is as enjoyable as it can be.

To do this, you need to complete two exercises. You should take your time, because this is the most important part of the plan. If you aren't clear about your destination, then you might end up driving in the wrong direction!

First, I want you to ask yourself what does the world look like when I'm gone? Work your way through the following checklist:

- How am I remembered? What do people say about me? What do they feel when they think of me?
- What are my loved ones' lives like now? Where do they live, and what do they do for a living? What kind of jobs do they have? How do they spend their free time?
- Who is benefitting from my wealth – friends, relatives, children, charities, schools and universities, my local community?
- Who is benefitting from my wisdom? What lessons and values have I left behind?
- Do I have any regrets? What's missing from this picture?
- What are the three most vital pieces of advice I want to leave for my loved ones?

These questions are designed to help you understand the destination of your journey. Don't worry too much about money at this stage – the point is to imagine your ideal scenario, then match it with reality so we can see what's possible. You should try to make the picture as detailed as you can. Talk to your friends and relatives about it, if you think it might help.

Next, I want you to ask what do the next 20 to 30 years of my life look like? Work through the following questions:

- Am I working? In what role, and for how long?
- Am I retired? If not, when will I retire, and how do I want to spend my time?
- Where do I live?
- How often do I go on holiday, and where?
- What role do I have in the lives of my children/ grandchildren?
- What are the main milestones I want to achieve over this period?

The point of this exercise is to show you how you want the rest of your life to unfold. This is important, because your legacy will depend on the decisions you make in the years ahead, and vice versa. One of the biggest benefits of planning for the end of your life is that it helps you see how much you've still got ahead of you!

Take your time with these activities. The picture you paint doesn't have to be too complicated or grand, but it has to be clear in your mind. Once you're happy with what you see, you're ready to move on to the next step.

Step Two: Where are you today?

After you've entered your destination into your sat-nav, the first thing it does is to find your current location. Once the satnav has pinpointed where you are, it can show you the best route to your goal. This is the whole point of Step Two – helping you see where you are today, so that you can understand what you need to do to make your vision a reality.

This means getting a clear view of your current financial situation – income, expenses, savings, assets and liabilities. This can be a complicated process, but the good news is that people often find out that they have more wealth than they realise! With the right help, you can find value in places you never thought to look. I'll explain more about how to do this in the next chapter.

Once we've got an overall picture of where you are today, we can compare it to the vision you created in Step One and see how well they match. It's now that the work of planning really begins. By understanding your current resources, we can start to prioritise. Which parts of your vision are most important, and how close are you to achieving them? What do we need to do to lay the foundation for your legacy?

Now we're ready to start looking at the journey itself. Which is the smoothest, fastest route to your destination, and which wrong turns do we need to avoid?

Step Three: What are your risks?

A good satnav doesn't simply show you the shortest path to your goal. It also uses real-time data to help you avoid traffic jams and busy stretches of road, as well as steering you away from accidents, fallen trees, floods and so on. Similarly, your plan is there to help you spot and avoid the risks that might prevent you from reaching your destination.

In my professional experience, I've found that many people don't like to talk about risk. When I talk to married people about planning for their future, I often hear the same thing: "It's simple. I just want to leave everything to my spouse and children." "That's fine," I reply, "but have you thought about the risks?" This usually gets a blank look. I get it – out of sight, out of mind, right?

But think about it this way – how would you try to avoid driving your car into a pothole? By closing your eyes and pretending that there's nothing but smooth tarmac ahead of you? Or keeping your gaze fixed on the road and steering carefully around the danger? The best way to manage risk is to be honest and open about what could go wrong.

With a clear picture of your current finances, we'll be able to build a personalised risk profile. This will identify the biggest financial dangers which could prevent you from passing on your wealth to the people who really deserve it. These could include:

• How close are you to the inheritance tax threshold (it's probably nearer than you think!)?
• What happens if you become seriously ill?
• What happens if you die, and your spouse remarries?
• What happens if your children get divorced?
• Is there a chance your children could squander their inheritance?

As you can see, risk can come at you from many different angles! There's no need to feel overwhelmed, though. With the support of a qualified estate planner, you can break down your risk into manageable packages, and find the best strategy to keep it minimised.

Step Four: What are your solutions?

This is it! You've entered your destination into the satnav, pinpointed your current location and highlighted your biggest risks. Now it's time to choose your route.

The solutions you require will be highly personal, depending on your vision, your financial situation and your risk profile. The most important decision facing you is making sure you get the right help. People often assume that estate planning is as simple as writing a will, but as I've tried to show in the rest of this chapter, there's far more to it than that.

Remember – you're making a plan for your whole life, and life is complex! The more assets you have, and the more protection you want for yourself and your family, the more complex your plan becomes.

You might think you've got the situation under control, but unforeseen events – like a small rise in asset prices pushing you over the inheritance tax threshold – can throw everything out of whack. You need to make sure you've got every outcome covered.

This is why it is so important to engage a professional estate planner. It's the job of professionals to demystify complexity in their chosen field, so the rest of us can focus on the roles that suit us best.

In the estate planning business, our solutions usually come in two types. First is Death Planning. These are measures that will kick in the moment that you pass away, making sure that your wealth is protected and that it finds its way to the right people. We usually focus on getting these set up as quickly as possible, just in case something unfortunate happens in the meantime!

Second is Lifetime Planning. These are long-term strategies designed to help you build your legacy over the long term. They involve addressing any potential tax issues, organising your property and assets in the most efficient way, and looking at the structure of your business to ensure that your family stands to benefit in the event of your passing. By combining these two approaches, we make sure you have a plan that covers you right now and in the future.

To see how these four steps can play out in practice, here's another case study from my archives.

Case Study: Malcolm and Alison

Malcolm and Alison are a couple in their mid-seventies with an estate worth several million pounds. They came to Sure Wealth after realising that their wealth could be vulnerable to serious tax liabilities if they both passed away in the next few years.

Defining your vision: Malcolm and Alison have worked hard their whole lives to build up a substantial estate to share with their descendants. Their children are now in their fifties, and the grandkids are growing up fast, so it's time to make sure everything is in place so that their loved ones get the benefit of their generosity.

Malcolm and Alison are also big believers in prudence and good financial planning, and want to ensure that these values are passed on to the next generation.

Where are you today: The majority of Malcolm and Alison's wealth is now held in the form of several buy-to-let properties, which are now mortgage free. They also own their own residence, two cars, extensive savings and a range of personal valuables.

What are your risks: If Malcolm and Alison both passed away unexpectedly, their estate could be subject to an inheritance tax bill upwards of £400,000. There is also the risk that without a detailed plan, their wealth might not make it to their intended recipients.

What are your solutions: After a detailed investigation of Malcolm and Alison's financial situation, I created a personalised plan including the following provisions:

Rewritten wills including detailed instructions for the transfer of all assets and comprehensive protections against taxation and misallocation of wealth.

Setting up lasting powers of attorney, giving their children the right to make decisions on Malcolm and Alison's behalf in the event that they become mentally incapacitated.

Robust trust structures which will protect both their money and their properties from third-parties, minimising tax liabilities and ensuring that these assets are passed on to their children.

Lifetime gifting of their excess wealth to minimise their inheritance tax bill.

We'll look more closely at the solutions described above in a later chapter. Next, we're going to think a bit more deeply about the subject of wealth. What is wealth? How do I measure it? How much do I have? You might find yourself pleasantly surprised by the answer!

Chapter 4

You are Wealthier than You Realise

"Wealth is the ability to fully experience life."

--Henry David Thoreau

What am I worth?

Before you set your life plan in motion, you need to know what you've got to work with. How much wealth do you have to pass on to your descendants? In my experience, most people have more than they think – it's simply a case of knowing the right places to look!

First, though, we need to acknowledge that wealth can be a tricky subject to discuss, especially with strangers. Sometimes, we even hide the truth of the situation from ourselves! By putting our heads in the sand, we think we're saving ourselves stress and hassle, though we're really making things worse in the long run. The only way to take the worry out of wealth is through open, honest discussions with your estate planner.

It's the job of your estate planner to help you feel comfortable talking about your wealth. This requires trust, and trust can't be magicked out of thin air – it has to be built. One of the signs of a good estate planner is that they're interested in more than just your money. They'll want to get to know you as a person, to understand your family, your priorities and your values. By doing this, they are building the foundation of a trusting relationship.

The best way you can help them is to be as open with them as possible, both on financial and non-financial matters! With a wider understanding of what wealth means to you and your family, your advisor will be able to tailor their support to your specific needs. The more you disclose, the better the quality of the advice you'll receive.

In the following pages, I'm going to provide a checklist that will give you a snapshot of your estate as it currently stands. I want you to work through it step by step. Think of it as a chance to be completely honest with yourself, to put everything out on the table. Your goal should be to get yourself to a place where you feel comfortable sharing this snapshot with a professional. This preparation will make it much easier to build openness and trust between you and your advisor.

What is wealth?

There are two ways of answering this question. The first is that your wealth is equal to your net worth. Your net worth can be calculated through a simple equation.

Net Worth = Total Assets − Total Liabilities

What does this mean? It's simple really. When you pass away, your net worth is the value of all the assets you own, minus all your liabilities. This figure is used to calculate how much tax you owe. Once the taxman has taken his cut, whatever's left will be distributed according to the instructions left in your will.

What about the second meaning of wealth? This is a little more complicated, but just as important. Wealth is not just money, material goods, assets and liabilities. It's also a mindset. Having a wealth mindset means being able to look at yourself in the mirror and understand your own true value.

All of us have one great source of wealth that no-one else can take away – our skills, our knowledge and our experience. These are the qualities that won you the success you've had throughout your life, as well as your future earning potential. They are what make you a wealth-generating machine! When you start to look at things this way, you'll realise that wealth – and the sources of future wealth – are all around you.

With the right mindset, you'll find it much easier to identify sources of wealth in your life that might otherwise have slipped your mind – your passion for art, or fine wine, for example. You'll also find that planning for your own death doesn't mean putting a full stop at the end of your life story. It's also about finding new ways to enrich and support your family for decades to come.

Calculating your net worth

Over the next few pages, I'm going to take you through a series of steps that will help you get a rough snapshot of your net worth. We're talking about a ballpark figure here – if you want more precise numbers, you should contact me directly for a detailed breakdown. The point of this exercise is to empower you to approach that conversation with confidence. It should be a straightforward process, but it'll take time and patience to make sure you haven't left anything out.

Calculating your net worth involves three basic steps:

1 – What are my assets?

2 – What are my liabilities?

3 – What's my tax situation?

Once these steps are complete, you'll have a good idea of where your net worth stands. Then you can start planning how to use it to realise your vision for your legacy.

Step One: What are my assets?

What do we mean by an asset? Quite simply, an asset is anything that has a monetary value attached to it. This means cash and any property that could be sold for cash, including those precious objects that you'd never dream of parting with. Even though you'd never in a million years consider selling that antique vase or the ring you inherited from your grandmother, they still count as part of your estate.

It's important to be as thorough as possible here. If you're hesitating over whether to include a piece of property among your assets, you probably should, just to be on the safe side. In my experience, most people tend to undervalue their assets, either because they overlook valuable pieces of property or because they underestimate their worth. Remember, the price of many assets appreciates over time, so any old valuations you have may be out of date.

To keep things simple, I've organised the following list into the most important asset categories. Work your way through, including everything that comes to mind. Remember, everything you include is a potential source of future wealth for your family! Approximate values are good enough here – your advisor will help you pin down more accurate numbers when the time is right.

Property and real estate

What is the value of your main residence? Have you paid off your mortgage?

What is the value of any other properties you own – second homes, holiday homes, rentals?

Savings and investments

What is the value of your investments – stocks, shares, bonds, securities?

What is the value of your savings?

Are you a creditor? If so, how much money are you owed and what are the terms of repayment?

Do you own any digital assets, such as cryptocurrencies? If so, what are their values and how can they be accessed?

Personal possessions

How many cars do you own, and what are they worth?

What valuable personal properties do you own? Think artwork, ornaments, antiques, jewellery, watches, luxury goods, vintage wines and premium spirits, high-end electronics, collectibles, memorabilia or instruments.

Business assets

Are you a business owner? If so, how is your business structured? Are you a director, or a partner? How many limited companies do you hold? Are you a shareholder? What is the value of your business(es)?

What assets does your business own? Is there a pay out upon the death of a director or shareholder?

Pensions and insurance

What is the value of your pension?

Do you have life insurance, and what is its value?

Are you entitled to any payments through work – for example, Death In Service, which employers and pension funds sometimes pay out if a person dies whilst still employed?

Foreign assets

Do you own any assets located in a foreign country or denominated in foreign currency?

Potential future earnings

Do you stand to receive any inheritances over the next 10 or 20 years? What amount?

Are you still at work? What is your projected income, and how long do you intend to work for?

Do your current assets, such as real estate or investments, stand to appreciate in value? By how much?

Don't worry if you can't fully answer all these questions right now. For some of them – particularly the ones about potential future earnings – you'll probably need professional help. The point is to give you a general idea of what's on the table. I bet you're already coming up with sources of wealth that might otherwise have slipped your mind.

Step Two: What are my liabilities?

Liabilities are anything that might reduce the value of your net worth, either before or after you die. We're talking debts, loan repayments, asset depreciation and other unforeseen circumstances.

Remember that any debts you owe when you pass away will be immediately subtracted from your estate before your will comes into effect, so it all comes out of your legacy. By pinpointing your liabilities, we can minimise these losses and make sure as much of your wealth as possible makes it to your family members and chosen causes.

Mortgages

For many people, their main liability will be their mort-gage. If you've paid yours off, you're in great shape – but remember to include outstanding mortgage payments on any secondary properties you might own.

Secured loans

A secured loan is money borrowed against the value of an asset you own. Mortgages are the most common example of a secured loan, but there are other kinds as well. Secured creditors get priority over unsecured creditors when debts are repaid from a person's estate.

Unsecured loans

Unsecured loans mean money borrowed without an asset to back it. It includes credit card debt, personal loans, leases, hire purchase and car finance.

Private loans

This is any money you've borrowed from friends, family or associates. Often, loans of this kind are done on a handshake, and backed by nothing but trust. That's fine, but if you pass away without settling these debts then your family may end up paying them out of their own pocket. By making sure these arrangements are properly documented, you can protect your family from this uncertainty.

Exposure to market volatility

The value of some of your assets – particularly real estate, investments and digital assets – can fluctuate according to market conditions. Remember the 2008 housing crash? It's important to know how exposed you are to events like this, so you and your family can plan for an uncertain future.

Jointly held assets

Do you hold a joint bank account with your partner, or have joint ownership of your home? Have you made arrangements for what happens if one of you passes away? Likewise, what happens to these joint assets if you get divorced? If you are divorced with children under the age of 18, you will need to plan to continue child maintenance payments even in the event of your death.

Gifts

One of the biggest benefits of having wealth is being able to be generous with it. As we get older, though, we have to make sure to keep a record of any substantial financial presents we make, because gifts given in the last seven years of our life can count towards our tax-free allowance.

If you can find a good response for each of these categories, then you'll have a pretty decent idea of your overall liabilities. Again, don't be too worried if there are questions you can't answer. Even more so than assets, calculating your liabilities is a complex job, and you'll need the help of a professional to get it right. You'll find the conversation much easier for having prepared yourself beforehand.

Step 3: What's my tax situation?

Now that you've got a rough picture of the value of your assets and your liabilities, you're ready for the fun part. How much tax do I owe? This is the flip side of the pleasant surprise that I was talking about earlier. When I tell my clients how much they're really worth, I'm rewarded with a 100-watt smile, but that happy expression soon turns itself upside down when they see their potential tax bill.

You should take that shock as a spur to act. Think about it – you're in a far better position now than you were 30 seconds ago, when you had no idea how much the taxman might grab. Forewarned, you can now take steps to make sure that you have maximum control over what happens to your wealth after you're gone. Once we know where you stand from a tax perspective, your advisor can work with you to design tax-efficient structures to conserve your legacy for future generations.

The benefits of knowing your worth

There are so many positives to getting a clear picture of your net worth. Working in this business, I get to see them every day. For one thing, there's the thrill of seeing just how well a lifetime of hard work has paid off. It's amazing to me how many people have no idea just how wealthy they are. Between you and me, I must have made more millionaires than Chris Tarrant. I never get tired of seeing the shock and pride on their faces.

You should also think of calculating your net worth as a piece of good housekeeping. By ensuring you have all your documents in order, you're saving trouble both for your future self, and for your executor, who will have the job of sorting through your things after you've gone. Do you want your grieving relatives spending days searching for lost files, passwords and safe keys, or do you want them to find everything laid out and ready to go?

Knowing how much you're worth gives you clarity, control and focus. You know what you need to do to deliver the vision laid out in your life plan, and you can start deciding how to divide your wealth between your inheritors. All the uncertainty and potential conflict that can come with a poorly organised estate can be prevented before it even becomes a problem, on your schedule and your terms.

Lastly, I want to correct a popular misconception about estate planning. I meet a lot of people who seem to think that good planning is all about having a hoarder's mentality – stashing your money away under your bed or at the bottom of the garden, never treating yourself or your family to a nice gift or a holiday, building up the biggest possible number in your bank account.

This couldn't be more wrong. In fact, hoarders often end up leaving less than they imagined, because so much of their legacy ends up going to tax. The real benefit of estate planning is that it gives you freedom. Once you know exactly what you're worth, you know how much you can afford to spend right now whilst still building your legacy. You want to give your family that dream holiday to the Maldives or Disney World? The choice is yours.

At the same time, once you've decided how much you want to leave to your descendants, what's to stop you from giving it to them now? Without proper planning, gifts like this can cause real trouble later on down the line, but you have a plan, and it covers every eventuality. If your daughter needs money for a house or car, why should she have to wait until you're gone? This way, you get to see the effects of your generosity with your own eyes. You can make your legacy while you're still here to witness it.

So far, this book has been all about you – the journey you're on, the wealth you possess, the legacy you want to leave behind. My goal has been to get you thinking positively about what can be, at the best of times, a difficult subject. I hope now that you have a clearer picture of the values you'd like to hand down to future generations, as well as an idea of how your existing wealth might contribute to that vision.

The next part of the book is going to focus more on the practical aspects of estate planning. Using the experience I've developed through my years on the job, I'm going to show you what best practice looks like, and the pitfalls you should avoid. By the time you've finished this book, you should know exactly what you need when looking for your perfect estate planner.

Chapter 5

What is Estate Planning?

"Plan for what is difficult while it is easy, do
what is great while it is small."

--Sun Tzu

Meet Kate and Toby

Kate and Toby are happily married with two children, Lily
(14) and Jack (10). Toby runs a successful marketing
firm which he co-owns with David, a friend from university. Kate is a journalist who writes for national maga-
zines and newspapers.

Kate and Toby live in a spacious four-bedroom house
in a small town in South East England. As well as their
home, they own two cars and a three-bedroom house
which they rent out. Between the two of them, they've

always made enough to live comfortably, and have plenty of savings in the bank.

One day, Toby gets into a serious car accident on the way to work. He is rushed to hospital, but unfortunately his injuries are too severe to be treated, and a few hours later he passes away with Kate by his side. As well as coping with this sudden, tragic loss, Kate now has to sort out Toby's estate. Did Toby leave all the right plans in place? Here are some of the questions Kate will need to answer:

- Should Toby's assets all go to Kate, or should they be shared with the children?
- What happens to Toby's business?
- What happens to their rental property?
- How much inheritance tax will be paid?
- What happens to Toby's estate if Kate should later remarry?
- Will Lily or Jack squander their inheritance, rather than using it for education or getting on the property ladder?

- Where are all Toby's documents kept? Does Kate know his passwords? What happens to his Facebook/ Apple/Microsoft accounts?
- Where are his digital assets – for instance, his Bitcoin wallet – and how can they be accessed?
- Who will manage the transfer of Toby's assets and do all the necessary admin?
- What happens with Toby's pension and life insurance policy?

I could go on, but that's probably enough to chew on for now! The reality is that there are a lot of hard questions to answer when a person passes away, and for under-standable reasons, family members are often not in the best shape to take on this work. When a loved one passes, we need space to grieve and to remember, not to be stressed and hassled with financial matters. But this stuff needs to be dealt with. This is why planning is so essential.

What is estate planning, and who needs it?

The point of estate planning is to find answers to all of these questions before they are needed. That way, when the moment comes, all the difficult decisions have already been made. All your relatives will need to do is to put your plan into motion, and your assets, values and wisdom will be transferred smoothly from one generation to the next.

Who needs an estate plan? It's simple – anyone with assets and people who depend on them.

I need to do a bit of myth-busting at this point. There's a strange assumption in this country that estate planning is only for the super-wealthy – multi-millionaires, aristocrats, landowners. If I ask you to think of someone with an estate, your mind will probably conjure up some kind of duke or baron, living in a stately home with an ornamental garden and a deer park.

But "estate" is just a legal term which means "all the stuff you own added together". Estates are like opinions – all of us have one! And as I keep saying, yours is probably worth more than you realise.

You may think of yourself as comfortably well-off, but not necessarily wealthy, but if you've completed the exercises from Chapter 4 you'll already have discovered that you have more assets than you first thought. It may not be up there with Jeff Bezos, but it's still a substantial amount, and you'll want to be in control of what happens to it after you're gone. This is what your estate plan is for.

The elements of an estate plan

Earlier in the book, I talked about how your life plan is like a satnav. It's how you decide where you want to go, and map out the route that will get you there. You could think of your estate plan as your car – the vehicle that will transport you to your destination.

Like a car, an estate plan is a mechanism made up of different parts. Each part serves a different function, but if you want the car to run smoothly, you'll want to make sure that every element of the machine is properly connected, so that they all work together. If your brakes aren't attached to the wheels, you won't get far before something goes wrong.

A solid estate plan will include the following elements:

- Professionally drafted wills
- Trusts
- Lasting Powers of Attorney
- Inheritance tax plan
- Business succession planning
- Secure document storage
- Funeral plan
- Probate plan
- Maintenance plan

Let's work through them one-by-one, and I'll show you how each element works as part of the overall mechanism of your estate plan.

Your will

Your will is the foundation of your estate plan. Think of it as the main body of the car – the chassis, wheels and engine. While you're alive, your will is dormant, but the moment you pass away it becomes active, ready to make sure that your legacy is delivered.

We might assume we all know what's supposed to go in a will, but it's important to be precise. A good will should cover all these bases:

- Who will be responsible for enacting your will when you're gone – your executor.
- Who will look after your children, if required – a guardian.
- What are your assets and who do they go to?

- Do you wish to make any gifts to individuals, charities or other bodies?
- What are your wishes for your funeral?

There are lots of different ways to make a will, some of them better than others. What's most important for you is that you know the difference between a good will and a bad will, so that you can be sure you're getting the right protection for your family. The first thing is to be sure that your will is drawn up by a professional, accredited by the Society of Will Writers (SWW) and the Society of Trust and Estate Practitioners (STEP). If you've been putting off getting your will sorted, don't hesitate any longer - get in touch with me today!

A good will is tailored to your vision of your legacy and be robust enough to stand up in court. It will contain a detailed breakdown of your assets, and will point to other legal structures which will ensure that your plan is carried out according to your wishes. It won't only show where you want your assets to go, but will provide ways to make sure they get there.

A bad will is a basic, boilerplate document, written by someone who hasn't looked deep enough into your vision and your goals. It will have an incomplete account of your assets, will have no instructions concerning how your legacy is to be used, and may not be up to date with the latest regulations. This last point is key – it's important to regularly refresh your will to make sure it covers any changes in the law.

Trusts

What is a trust, and what are they for? Well, there's a phrase we use in the estate planning business: "Wills direct, trusts protect."

Your will states where you want your assets to go. But it doesn't provide any guarantees as to how your money and property will be used. There's always the danger that your legacy could be squandered, or lost to debt, divorce or some other unforeseen event. A trust is a legal structure that will protect your legacy from these risks when you're no longer here to guide and support your family.

All types of assets can be held in a trust – money, real estate, personal property. Once the trust has been established, you decide who is allowed to access those assets and how. It might be that you don't want your children to receive their inheritance until they're 21 (or older!), or perhaps you want to make sure they use the money for a particular purpose, like putting down a deposit on a house.

After you've passed away, the trust will be managed by trusted people (known as trustees), chosen by you to make sure your wishes are fulfilled. This is how you protect your wealth from all the "what ifs" in life – because however much we love and believe in our family, we never know what might go wrong further down the road. By putting your assets in a trust, you can ensure that your wealth is passed on in a way that reflects your values and experience.

In our car metaphor, trusts are like the steering wheel. They give you control over where you want to go. A powerful engine is all well and good, but it's not much use if you can't choose which direction you're heading!

Lasting powers of attorney

Have you thought about who would carry out your wishes and make decisions on your behalf, if you ever lost the ability to do so yourself? From dementia, suffering a stroke or being involved in a car accident, our health can quickly deteriorate. Without the correct legal documents, neither your spouse or your family will be able to take decisions on your behalf if the worse were to happen. Making Lasting Powers of Attorney (LPA) in advance enables those people you trust to take care of your affairs one day. There are two kinds of LPA in the

UK - one covering Health and Welfare and one covering Property and Financial Affairs.

A Health and Welfare LPA allows a chosen individual to make important decisions about medical treatments and day-to-day care, including whether you should undergo major surgery and if or when to move you into a care home. A Property and Financial Affairs LPA allows that person to manage your finances, collect pensions or benefits and sell assets including your home. It's also possible to set up business-specific LPAs, nominating a partner or colleague to take business decisions on your behalf.

Of course this isn't a pleasant subject to dwell on, but what are the possible consequences of not setting up the appropriate LPAs?

Let's imagine Toby survived his car crash, but was put into a coma. It would be up to Kate to try and manage his finances and business affairs until he wakes up. Without power of attorney, she'd be fighting with one hand tied behind her back, lacking the authority to make the really important legal and financial decisions. An already stressful situation would be made a thousand times more difficult.

Powers of attorney are like your airbags. We all pray that we never have to use them, but if the worst happens we'll be so glad they're there.

Inheritance tax plan

A lot of people assume that inheritance tax won't be much of an issue for them, but with the growth in property values over the past few decades (particularly in the South East), most people's assets will qualify them for some kind of liability. If this is a problem for you, you'll need a plan to minimise your exposure.

Toby and Kate have a shared estate worth around £1.5 million. If Kate were to suddenly pass away, Lily and Jack would be facing a £200,000 liability on their inheritance. If, further down the line, they were to pass any of that money on to their children, it would be taxed all over again. Without a plan, hundreds of thousands of pounds will disappear from the family legacy.

It can be hard to predict how much inheritance tax you might have to pay. There are lots of factors involved – whether you're married or single, whether you have children, what kind of assets you hold. The only reliable way to find out how much you could end up paying is to consult with a professional advisor. They can then help you come up with a strategy to minimise your liabilities.

If you're unprepared, you could get into real trouble. If the government decides they want 40 per cent, then they're taking that 40 per cent, no matter what kind of assets you have. If they don't have the liquid cash, then your inheritors could be forced to refinance, take on debt or sell some of your assets in order to pay the inheritance tax. In a worst-case scenario, your wealth can end up creating extra financial stress for your family.

A good inheritance tax plan is like your car's mirrors. It lets you keep an eye on the hazards that might be coming up in your rearview, and take action before they become a risk to you and your family.

Business succession planning

As I mentioned earlier, Toby owns a successful marketing firm in partnership with his old friend David. They each hold a 50 per cent share in the company. When Toby passes away, his share of the business goes to his estate. His inheritors now own that 50 per cent stake, and that value must be realised one way or another. This can cause serious complications for David and the employees.

The simplest solution would be for David to buy out Toby's share of the business. But does he or the business have enough money to cover this purchase? If not, then David will need to find a new partner who can afford to buy Toby's share, or the company will have to be sold. If a suitable buyer isn't found in time, the business could collapse, costing everyone their jobs.

Another option would be that Kate steps in to run Toby's half of the business. This could work – but is this really what Kate wants? And how does David feel about this? Imagine the chaos for the employees, turning up to work every day with no idea if they'll still have a job.

Then there's the issue of Toby's role within the company. Before he passed away, Toby was always the more sales-oriented of the partners, responsible for bringing in most of the new business, whilst David handled the operational side. With Toby's expertise gone, investors and lenders may start to lose confidence that the company can maintain its levels of growth and performance.

It could also be that Toby has loaned money to the business, which must immediately be repaid on death. The company may be forced to take on debt in order to cover these repayments.

Fortunately, all these risks can be mitigated by good succession planning. Of course, there's really no way to replace a person with Toby's experience and expertise, but by sitting down together the two friends can make sure they've got contingencies in place should something go wrong. This will reassure their staff and lenders, and protect the value of the company going forward.

A business succession plan is like your car's onboard computer. It ticks along in the background, keeping an eye on your fuel usage, checking for engine faults and helping when you need to reverse or park. It's there to make sure things keep running smoothly so you can drive on with peace of mind.

Funeral plan

Funeral planning is highly personal. Some people can't bear thinking about it, others actually kind of enjoy it. As with all the other issues we've discussed in this book, it's better to face up to it than to bury your head in the sand, for your family's sake if nothing else. Ideally, this planning should be done together with your loved ones, since they'll be the ones carrying out your wishes.

Would you prefer a large ceremony, or a small, private affair? Religious or secular? What kind of music and readings would you like? Would you like there to be a wake? Who'll be responsible for organising, and how will they pay for it? If you want to pay for the funeral out of your estate you'll need to make arrangements for that.

Once you've decided what kind of funeral you want, it's important that your wishes are properly documented. This means that, whatever happens, your family will know what to do when the moment comes. I promise you – this will save your loved ones so much stress and hassle.

Your funeral plan is like heated car seats. You might not think of them as essential, but they make the ride so much more comfortable.

Secure document storage

So, you've laid all your plans and ensured that they're all properly documented. Where are you going to keep all that paperwork? Please don't tell me you're going to stuff them in that unmarked filing cabinet you keep in the garage or underneath the floor boards in the "secret safe" where nobody knows?

Your documents should be carefully labelled and stored, so that someone who doesn't know where they are (i.e., your executor) can find them without too much effort. A good estate planner will offer you a document storage solution which makes sure that copies of all your paperwork are kept safe until they are needed.

There are other items to be taken care of here, such as digital assets and passwords. Some estate planners now offer a digital estate planning facility, which will help you organise your digital profiles and properties as well as storing scanned copies of your documents which can be accessed by your family in the event of your death.

Document storage is like the spare tyre and toolkit you keep in the boot of your car. It's not flashy stuff, but you'll be glad it's there when you need it.

Probate plan

The loss of a family member, friend or someone close can be a difficult time. If you have been named as an executor for someone's estate, you will have the legal responsibility to distribute their estate in line with their wishes.

If you are not a financial expert, but have been asked to act as an executor for someone's estate, you may find probate confusing. You may not know how much tax there is to be paid, or may be unsure over your duties concerning the distribution of their assets or simply might not feel ready to deal with the complexities of administering an estate.

The probate process can vary in length depending on the complexity of the estate. It can be hard dealing with banks, pension companies and HMRC at the best of times, let alone when you are grieving. As an executor, you could be personally held liable for any mistakes such as:

- Not fully accounting for all assets and debts of the deceased
- Distributing the inheritance incorrectly
- Paying the wrong amount of tax
- Errors and delays in the submission of official documents

We recognise that immediately after a death, simple but practical advice is needed to avoid problems occurring or unwise action being taken.

That's why we have developed the Sure Wealth Assisted Probate Service, providing executors and trustees with the best support and expertise the whole way through the estate administration process. We will be holding your hand every step of the way through what can be a difficult time.

At Sure Wealth, we offer a fixed-fee probate service so our clients have full cost transparency. If your planner doesn't offer the same, you should ask them why!

Maintenance plan

The goal of every estate plan is to have clear, robust and up to date legal documents that result in a smooth transfer of your assets to your beneficiaries, at death or during your lifetime.

Just as your car requires an annual check up and MOT, you should regularly review your estate plan. There are a number of things which may change in the future that could affect your estate planning such as:

• Your health

• Your financial situation

• Life events such as marriage or divorce

• New born children or grandchildren

• Your beneficiaries circumstances

• Death in your family

- Your executor, trustees and guardian circumstances
- Any relevant changes in legislation and taxation

Far too often I have seen wills that were made 20 years ago and never been reviewed. Wealth levels have changed drastically and the children now adults. So many things can change in the space of a year, let alone a couple of decades! As wealth levels continue to surge, the last thing you also want to leave behind are disputes over the distribution of your wealth after death. There has been a significant increase in inheritance disputes in recent years and this risk can be minimised by ensuring your planning is kept up to date.

That's why at Sure Wealth we recently launched our Maintenance Plan. It is a proactive review service designed to help you maintain the value of your estate planning structure, as well as keeping your documents secure. When you set up your estate plan, you have made an investment of time your time and money into the financial security of your loved ones. Like any investment, it is essential to review it your estate plan on a regular basis to ensure it is valid and up to date.

Advice from an estate planner

There you have it – a quick snapshot of the main elements of an estate plan. This overview shows you the basic pieces you'll need to make sure your legacy is fully protected, but in order to get advice that you can really put into action, you should consult with a professional planner as soon as possible.

There are still a couple more tips I can give you right now though. The first is that it's never too soon to make your estate plan. Just like buying property, the best time to start is yesterday! You never know what might be around the corner. At a bare minimum you should sort out your will and power of attorney, but as our car metaphor shows, every part is needed if you want things to run smoothly.

Second: once you've made your estate plan, don't just file it away and forget. It needs to become a part of your routine planning. Just as you sit down every year to review your finances, you should do the same with your estate plans. Have you acquired any new assets or received a windfall? Did you get married or divorced? Has the law changed? All this needs to be priced in.

Third: don't see estate planning as a depressing task, but as a way to free yourself to make the most of the rest of your life whilst taking care of any future uncertainties. As I always say: Plan like you could die tomorrow, act like you could live forever.

Chapter 6

The Risks of Passing On Your Wealth

"Expect the best. Prepare for the worst.
Capitalize on what comes."

--Zig Ziglar

Murphy's Law

We've covered a lot of ground over the last five chapters, so let's take a minute and recap. You've learned that facing up to your own mortality can be an empowering experience, and you've seen the value of building a legacy. You've understood the importance of having a plan, and grasped the concept of wealth, discovering that you have more of it than you realise. You've even glimpsed some of the technicalities of estate planning.

By now, you probably feel like you're ready to go, and if you've followed the path I've laid out, you're actually quite well prepared. You have a clear idea of what your legacy means to you, you've identified your main sources of wealth and you've started putting together a plan. But let's not be too hasty. Before you set off trying to put your own affairs in order, it's important that we understand the scale of the risks involved.

Like all good estate planners, I'm a big believer in Murphy's Law – "Anything that can go wrong, will go wrong." Not because I'm a pessimistic guy, but because it's my job to make sure my clients are prepared for every outcome. You might not want to think too hard about all the risks and hazards that could stop you passing your wealth on to the next generation, but life is made up of "what ifs". What use is a plan that falls apart at the first sign of crisis?

To put it another way: You should plan like a pessimist, so you can live like an optimist. The process of going through worst-case scenarios can be uncomfortable, but the benefit you reap will be worth it – true peace of mind. In this chapter, we're going to cover all of the major "what ifs" that life might throw at you, and show how they can be factored into your plan.

Remarriage

Earlier on, I mentioned the most common thing I hear when couples come to me to discuss their estate: "I just want to leave everything to my spouse." On an emotional level this makes total sense, but very rarely do people consider the dangers that come with this distribution. One of the biggest is the risk of remarriage.

Today, the average UK life expectancy is roughly 79 years for males, 83 years for females. If you pass away in your 50s or 60s, your spouse probably has another 20 to 30 years of living ahead of them. In that time, there's a pretty good chance they'll meet somebody else that they'd like to spend their time with. For many of us, this can be a comforting thought. If the worst should happen to us, we wouldn't want our partner to go through the rest of their life alone.

However happy you might be for your spouse to find love again after you're gone, this can pose serious risks to your legacy. Should they remarry, their new partner will then have access to their wealth. This means that half – or more – of the assets you left could end up in the hands of a person you do not know.

Of course, it could be that your spouse's new partner is considerate and respectful enough to make sure that your legacy continues to be used according to your wishes. But let's assume that they aren't. What could happen?

- If your spouse and your new partner divorce, the latter could walk off with half of your legacy.
- If your spouse has an accident or becomes seriously ill, their new partner could acquire power of attorney, giving them full control of your legacy.

- If your spouse passes away, then your legacy could pass to their new partner.
- If you and your spouse have children, then they could end up being disinherited, with your wealth passing instead to their new stepparent.

Family life has evolved over the past 30 years. As divorce has become more common, so has remarriage. When people remarry, they may bring with them children from their previous relationships, creating a new "blended family". These blended families often get along fine, but from an inheritance point of view, they can be an absolute nightmare.

Let's say that you and your partner have two young children. Five or six years after you've died, your spouse remarries someone with three children of their own. Unfortunately, your kids and their new stepparent don't get along too well. A few years further down the line, your spouse also passes away, leaving your legacy in the hands of the stepparent from hell. Who do you think is going to see more of that money – your kids, or their stepsiblings?

We don't have to use our imagination to picture how situations like this play out. They're on our screens every day, in shows like Game of Thrones and Succession and films like Marriage Story, while the newspapers are full of tales of family feuds pitting stepparents against children. Sad as it is to admit it, stuff like this happens every day. It could happen to you.

The only way to protect your family and your legacy from these risks is to make sure your estate plan contains the right legal structures. Using trusts, for example, you can make sure that only certain people have the right to access your wealth, and only for purposes you've approved. Taking measures like these doesn't mean that you don't love or trust your partner; instead, it shows your desire to keep caring for your family even when you're no longer physically present.

Protecting your children

Young people have it hard these days. Skyrocketing house prices, student debt and a tough job market can make it difficult for them to achieve stability and security. Climate change, Covid-19 and other global issues create anxiety about the future. Meanwhile, social media and influencer culture creates pressure to get rich quick and flaunt your wealth by splurging on cars, fashion and jewellery.

Under these circumstances, we all want to do whatever we can to help our children. But is leaving them a big pile of money and assets the best way to do it? Unfortunately, the pressures of growing up in the 21st century can mean that our kids are not always in the best place to use wealth wisely. Your legacy could end up paying off debts, buying a flash car or being gambled on cryptocurrency. Are you ok with that?

Material things are only one part of the legacy we leave to our children. There's also our knowledge and values.

We all do our best to pass our experience on to the next generation, but once we're no longer around, they're on their own, right? Well, not exactly. With effective trust planning, our wisdom can continue to guide our kids for decades after our passing.

This means creating the legal structures which ensure that your children only get their inheritance when they're ready to use it. This can be tied to age, or to specific milestones such as buying their first property or being employed for a certain length of time. If your wealth is held in a limited company, then your children can be awarded shares which provide dividends, but not voting rights, until they've proved they're up for that kind of responsibility.

There are many different risks which could lead to your children misusing or losing access to your wealth. I'm going to list just a few below:

Vulnerability

It might be that you have a child who is vulnerable in one way or another – disability, illness, addiction. They might just be the kind of person who is prone to making bad decisions, or who surrounds themselves with the wrong friends.

In cases like these, the best way to support your kid may not be to give them everything in one go, but to make sure that their inheritance is staggered to support their needs over the longer term. You also need to appoint the right people to watch over your wealth and make sure it's being used in your child's best interests.

Expectations of inheritance

It's a sad fact that the expectation of inheritance can affect the way that some young people live their lives. The knowledge that a big pay day is waiting over the horizon can lead some to reckless living, counting on the bailout from their parents, whilst in others it can result in a lack of ambition.

You grafted hard to accumulate your wealth; with the right measures you can ensure that your children emulate your work ethic, rather than sitting back and waiting for your money to trickle down.

Debt and bankruptcy

As it gets harder to maintain a stable career, more and more young people are turning to entrepreneurship to make a living. This could mean many things, from starting their own small business to trading cryptocurrency online. On the other hand, as your sons and daughters get older they may want to trade the security of their corporate job for something more exciting or fulfilling.

As parents, we want to support our children in everything they do, especially when they're trying to better themselves. However, we also need to be conscious of the facts.

Almost two-thirds (60 per cent) of new businesses fail in the first three years. Do you want your money to be subsidising that kind of risk? It could result in your legacy ending up in the hands of creditors. When a bank goes to recover what it's owed from a debtor's account, they don't care about where the money came from.

If you decide you want to support your children in their business ventures, there are ways to structure things so that the whole of your wealth isn't exposed at once. In high-level investment, investee companies often have to go through several funding rounds, where they must hit pre-set targets to unlock the next pot of cash. You can do something similar with your legacy, making sure that if your kid's business goes belly up, they won't lose their whole inheritance.

Similarly, you might have a child who has already incurred substantial debts. They might even be counting on using their inheritance to pay them off. In this case, do you want to leave them one lump sum that immediately disappears into their creditor's pockets? Or do you want to create a structure which allows you to help your child sustainably over the long term, while protecting your wealth from third parties?

Divorce

We've spoken about what can happen if your spouse remarries and then gets divorced, but what about your children? This is another way that your legacy can end up outside of your family. Are you comfortable with your ex-son or ex-daughter-in-law getting hold of your wealth? With the right measures, you can ensure that your legacy is only accessible to your immediate family.

Giving your wealth away while you're still alive

I often meet clients whose greatest desire is to give everything away to their kids while they're still alive. This means that they no longer have to deal with the hassle of owning expensive assets, while also getting to see their children enjoy the fruits of their generosity. There's nothing wrong with giving gifts, but you have to make sure they've been factored into your plan, and that all the risks have been properly accounted for.

Obviously, I'm always pleased to hear people making plans for what the world will look like without them. Giving wealth away to your kids is a big part of that. But remember – you could have another 10, 20, or 30 years of living ahead of you. If you let go of too much all at once, then you've just given away your independence.

For instance, I've known several people who wanted to turn over ownership of their main residence to their children. But what happens if something goes wrong in your life, or theirs? If you run into financial difficulty, your house is potentially an asset you can borrow against. On the other hand, if your child goes bankrupt while owning the deeds to your residence, then your home could easily end up in the hands of creditors. Then where are you supposed to live?

The main lesson here is to be prudent in your gift giving. Don't let generosity get the better of good judgement, and remember that part of your planning is making sure you have enough to live out the rest of your days in comfort.

Care fees

The good news is that today, most people in this country are living longer lives. The bad news is that this means that past a certain point, ill health becomes increasingly likely. If you're unlucky, you may find yourself in a condition where you can no longer look after yourself, and the care burden becomes too much for your family. In this case, you'll need to pay for professional help.

Just like death and taxes, this is one of those things that can't be avoided, but it can be factored into your plan. Care costs can vary a lot, along with the quality of the care you'll receive. Will you want support in your home, or would you be more comfortable in a specialised residence? It's best to start thinking about this now, so that the costs can be covered in advance.

Your estate planner should be able to put you in touch with a specialist care planner who will be able to walk you through your options and help find the best solution for you and your family.

Of course, the risks listed above are far from exhaustive. Other risks to consider include business risk and inheritance tax, which I discussed in the previous chapter. The risks you'll face will be personal to you and your circumstances, which is why you'll need professional support to make sure you don't overlook any blind spots.

Getting the right help

It's possible you might feel a bit overwhelmed after the last two chapters. I get it – it's a lot of information to take in. You shouldn't worry too much, though, because you don't have to deal with all that complexity on your own.

A good estate plan is like a well-oiled machine. My goal has been to help you recognise the different parts, so that you can tell if something important is missing. The job of getting that machine purring belongs to your estate planner. In the following chapters, I'm going to give you some insider tips on how to make sure you find the right planner for your legacy.

Chapter 7

Investing in Your Family's Future

"Someone is sitting in the shade today because
someone planted a tree a long time ago."

--Warren Buffet

The great wealth transfer

Right now, we're living through the single biggest transfer of generational wealth in world history. Over the next
decade the baby boomers – people born between 1946
and 1964 – will pass on more than £30 billion in cash
and assets to their millennial descendants.

This is a mind-blowing stat – and a bittersweet one too.
On the one hand it's an unwelcome reminder that many
of us aren't getting any younger! On the other hand, it
should be a cause for great pride and satisfaction. A

generation of parents are handing their legacy – the product of 40 or 50 years of hard graft – down to their children, offering them a leg-up in what are increasingly tough times.

However, there's a crisis brewing behind that huge number, and not enough people are talking about it. A 2017 report by the King's Court Trust found that almost 30 per cent of British adults over the age of 55 did not have a proper will in place. Of the people who do, it's likely that the majority have a standard generic document, without the tailored protections I've described in previous chapters. Across the overall population, 61 per cent of people had no will of any kind.1

A survey by the financial services company Sanlam found that two-thirds of people over the age of 55 are concerned that the younger generation is not receiving

---

1   Kings Court Trust, *A Changing Landscape: The Will Writing Industry in 2017*, 2017, https://www.kctrust.co.uk/partners/will-writer-research. See also Kings Court Trust, *Wealth Transfer in the UK: The continuing story of the inheritance economy*, 2017, https://tinyurl.com/ye6cd9vu.

the right financial advice. The same report also found that 40 per cent of people between the ages of 25 and 40 struggle to engage with the task of financial planning, and 38 per cent of under-40s have not even discussed the issue with their benefactors.2

This is a massive risk. Without the proper structures in place, there's a real chance that billions of pounds could disappear down the drain, whether that's to inheritance tax, debt, or divorce and other family issues. It's essential that both sides of the Great Wealth Transfer – both the elder and younger generations – make sure they're getting the right advice, or else the baby boomers could see their legacy squandered before it's had time to flourish.

---

2   Sanlam, *The Generation Game*, 2018, https://tinyurl.com/yc5bvh4y. See also Marteen Micheau, "Preparing For The 'Great Wealth Transfer'", *Sanlam*, https://sanlamprivatewealth.sanlam.com/resources/fiduciary-tax/preparing-for-the-great-wealth-transfer/.

Inheritance in the information age

In recent years at least, there has never been a more dangerous time to pass on your wealth. Covid-19, Brexit and global instability have created insecurity for businesses and uncertainty for investors. Assets that would have been a safe bet just a few years ago are now looking a lot riskier. The punishments for financial failure are bigger than ever – but how do we make sure that we don't make the wrong choices for ourselves and our family?

Information isn't the problem. Thanks to the internet, ordinary people have more financial data at their fingertips than at any other time in human history. This has created a new DIY culture in finance. Many people no longer use stockbrokers to manage their investments; instead, they do their own online research, following tips from social media influencers and using apps like eToro to trade stocks and shares.

I'm not judging anyone for using online investment to make a little passive income. If you're smart, there's certainly money to be made. However, if this DIY attitude is applied to estate planning, then we're really flirting with disaster. You can't secure your legacy and safeguard your family's future by watching a couple of YouTube videos and following a wikiHow tutorial.

Let's take an analogy we can all relate to. Imagine that for the past few days you've been feeling a bit under the weather. Nothing too awful, but the symptoms are kind of strange – a fuzzy feeling in your head, stickiness in your throat, pains in the small of your back. You're too busy to get proper medical advice, but you are a bit worried, so you decide to consult our good friend Doctor Google.

You type your symptoms into the search bar and follow a couple of links to professional-looking medical advice pages. Naturally a bit of a worrier, you're drawn to the most exotic-sounding diagnoses. One disease in particular catches your attention. Your eyes start to water, and your palms get sweaty. Before you know it, two hours have flown by and you've convinced yourself you've got inoperable brain cancer.

We've all been there, right? It's so easy to end up going down a rabbit hole and getting yourself all worked up over nothing. The problem is that for people without the right expertise, it can be hard sometimes to sort the rubbish from the gold. I'm no doctor – to me, one piece of medical advice looks just as good as another.

The exact same thing can happen when you Google "how to write a will" or "how to manage inheritance tax". You'll find plenty of information out there, but how do you tell the straight shooters from the con artists? How do you know which advice is right for your unique situation? One big risk is that you end up overloaded and overwhelmed, which can push you into a cycle of procrastination. Another is that you make the wrong choice for you and your family.

Again, think about your health. If it turns out, God forbid, that you do have brain cancer, how would you choose to handle it? Would you try to do brain surgery on yourself, or ask your physio or your personal trainer to give it a whirl?

I certainly hope not! What I'd hope you'd do is to contact a professional brain surgeon, someone with decades of experience treating your specific condition. Estate planning should be no different.

What your estate planner can do for you

Estate planning may not quite be on the same level as brain surgery, but still, a qualified planner is an expert who has spent years honing their craft. Like any other professional, they've worked hard to become masters of the technical details, so you don't have to be. Your mechanic understands how your car engine works, so all you need to do is get in and drive. An estate planner is like a mechanic for your financial legacy.

Below, I'm going to list some of the main benefits a good estate planner will bring to you. Remember though that these are just general pointers! Your estate planner will provide support and advice that is specially tailored to your unique circumstances. The only way for you to discover the value they could bring is to give them a call and start the conversation.

Your estate planner cuts through the noise

The first thing your estate planner will do is cut through all the noise, giving you the advice that applies directly to your situation and leaving the rest to Google. They already know everything you could find online, and they've done you the favour of pre-filtering everything for clickbait and spam. Instead, you'll get a practical, step-by-step plan designed to fulfil your vision.

Your estate planner offers a bespoke service

The problem with even the best DIY online services is that they can only give you a generic, cookie-cutter approach. Your estate planner will help you craft a strategy that is specific to your needs. A good estate planner will want to get to know you and your family on a deep personal level, so they can really understand your values and vision, and respond with the best possible guidance.

Your estate planner will protect the future of your business

For business owners, your estate planner will ensure that your business continues to prosper and grow even when you're not there to lead it in person. We've highlighted a few different ways this can be achieved throughout this book, including succession planning and lasting powers of attorney. This will guarantee that even in the case of an unforeseen tragedy, your business will keep on delivering value for your clients and generating wealth for your family and colleagues for decades to come.

Your estate planner is in it for the long term

A good planner will be looking to engage you in a long-term relationship. This is because the arrangements you make together are designed to last for decades to come. If your estate plan is a good one, it will outlive you, and maybe even your children as well, as they use it as the template to pass their wealth on to your grandchildren. The very best estate planners will have this multi-generational vision in mind from the moment you first meet.

Your estate planner will challenge you

Unlike qualified estate planners, a solicitor or will writer will not necessarily be an expert in planning financial legacies. Their role is more to act as a translator, taking your wishes and putting them in the right legal language.

The guidance will be limited to dotting 'i's and crossing 't's – if it turns out you've made a mistake in your financial planning, they might not be in a position to point it out.

An estate planner, on the other hand, will have strong opinions about what's best for you and your legacy, and they won't be afraid of sharing them. Whilst they will always be respectful and sensitive to your needs, don't be surprised if your planner challenges your decisions every now and again. Their duty is to provide the best possible guidance for you and your family, and sometimes this means asking you to think twice about your initial assumptions.

Your estate planner will choose the right tools for the job

The difference between a financial advisor and an estate planner is like the difference between your GP and your cardiologist. One is a generalist, qualified to support you with everyday issues; the other has a particular skill set designed to address a specific problem. When it comes to securing your legacy, you'll need the specialist knowledge of a qualified estate planner to deliver the best results.

Having said that, every family's situation is unique, and it's unlikely that any estate planner will have the full range of experience necessary to meet your needs. A good estate planner will know when it's time to consult with an outside expert, and what's more, they'll know who to call. Tax advisers, accountants, stockbrokers, care experts, business solicitors – whatever the circumstances, your estate planner should have the right contacts.

In this way, you can think of your estate planner as the conductor of an orchestra. Each individual musician only knows their own part, but the conductor sees the entire score, and lets each section of the orchestra know when it's their turn to join in. Likewise, because your estate planner knows your strategy from back to front, they understand exactly when the time is right to bring other players into the picture.

Your estate planner will provide holistic solutions

The guidance offered by your estate planner will be based not just on their experience and expertise, but also on a deep understanding of your personal aspirations, motivations and values, your family dynamics and relationships, and the structure of your assets and finances. Together, you will craft a holistic plan which reflects the unique personalities of you and your family as well as your particular financial circumstances.

I've talked a lot about the value that an estate planner can bring, but really it's this last point which sets them apart from other financial and legal professionals. No-one else will be able to provide you with a plan that can deal with all the crazy, wonderful, joyful complexities that mean that your family is like no other on the face of this Earth.

Estate planning is an investment in your future

Let's get this out in the open – like any other professional, estate planners charge a fee for the services they provide. How much is a choice for each individual practitioner, but you can expect the cost to reflect the years of hard work that have gone into making the planner the expert he or she is today.

Now, it's true that I may be a little biased on this subject, but my advice to all families is that they should see this expenditure not as a cost, but as an investment. After all, at the end of the day a good estate planner will create value for you and your family far in excess of their fee. Like any other investment, engaging an estate planner should be seen as an opportunity to grow your wealth. Here are just some of the ways this can happen:

Future-proofing your wealth: As we've explored through-out this book, there are all sorts of unforeseen events that can threaten your wealth as it passes down through the generations. For example, the divorce of one of your beneficiaries can put up to 50 per cent of your legacy at risk. How much would you pay to protect half of your fortune for years to come?

Creating tax-efficient structures: The value that can be gained from inheritance tax strategies will vary from cli-ent to client, but it's not unusual for an outlay of around £5,000 to result in savings in the region of £200,000 or even £300,000. Not a bad return on investment, I think you'll agree!

Generational wealth planning: Some of the richest fam-ilies in this country have trust funds which are decades, or even centuries old. This is because they understand that real wealth is created on a generational scale. An estate planner can help you organise your assets so they continue to appreciate in value year on year, providing a resource that will support your descendants after you, your children and even their children are long gone.

Nurturing your intangible assets: I've spoken a lot in this book about the true meaning of legacy. Legacy is not just material wealth, but the knowledge, experience and values we pass on to future generations. In the preceding chapters, I've tried to show how you can embed these intangibles into the design of your estate plan, meaning that your wisdom will go on guiding your descendants even after you're no longer there to help them.

You can't put a price on values or wisdom, but this doesn't mean that they won't have material benefits for your inheritors! By leaving structures behind which help them make better financial decisions, you'll be supporting them in protecting and growing their wealth in the years ahead.

Think of the pride and satisfaction that comes with knowing your family is set up for decades to come. A good estate plan isn't just for what happens after you're gone, it's also about allowing you to experience this peace of mind right now and for the rest of your time on this planet.

Chapter 8

Finding The Perfect Estate Planner

"He who walks with the wise grows wise, but
a companion of fools suffers harm."

--Proverbs 13:20

By this point you should be ready to begin your journey towards creating your own estate plan. You understand the basic concepts of legacy, wealth and risk, and you've explored how they apply to you and your family.

The next step is most important – choosing your estate planner. This is the person who is going to deliver your legacy to your beneficiaries, so you've got to make sure you get it right. After all, most of us don't get the chance to die twice!

Think about the legacy vision you've pieced together over the course of this book. Your estate planner must know that vision inside out. They'll have to understand the values that are driving your plan, and they'll need to know your family almost as well as their own. There will be moments where you and your estate planner will have to confront uncomfortable truths – both about your own passing, and the future risks that could endanger your legacy.

Clearly, choosing an estate planner is a highly personal decision. You will need to use your judgement to pick the right person for you and your family. Your criteria must reflect the qualities you think are needed to deliver your vision. However, there are still a few general requirements that apply in all cases. Here's a checklist to help steer your decision making.

Qualifications and insurance

The highest accreditations for estate planners are awarded by STEP (the Society of Trust and Estate Planners). A STEP qualification shows that this planner has been approved by the most prestigious global professional body for multi-generational wealth planning. If your estate planner isn't a certified member of STEP, then you can't be sure you're getting the best available service.

Other important memberships include the Society of Will Writers and the Society of Trust and Estate Practitioners. These show that a planner is well regarded by their peers and is trained in important fundamentals, like will writing. They should also hold professional indemnity insurance to cover any unforeseen outcomes.

Personal profile

As I explained in the previous chapter, a good estate planner needs to understand you and your family on a deep level – your day-to-day motivations, your long-term ambitions, your characters, your relationships and your points of tension. They will also be looking to work with you over the long term.

This means it's essential that you are a good fit person-ality-wise. It probably doesn't matter if you don't really like your dentist or your solicitor, but if you don't get on with your estate planner, this could turn into a real prob-lem later on down the line! Here are some questions you can ask yourself to discover whether a particular planner is the right fit for you:

- Do you feel like you connect with your planner? Does he or she make you feel comfortable, particularly when discussing touchy subjects like death, divorce or family conflict?
- Are they a good listener? Do they give you room to speak and show by their responses that they've absorbed your words?

- Do they understand your values and vision? Do you think they could explain your legacy vision to a stranger if you weren't there to help them?
- Would you feel happy to introduce your planner to your family and friends? If you have, did they get along?
- Do you value their advice? When they make a suggestion, are you inclined to take it seriously?
- Do you trust them? Do you find it easy to be honest and open with them about your finances and family relationships?
- Will they get along with your children and any other future beneficiaries? Can you see them as your trusted family advisor for decades to come?

Professional relationship

As well as feeling comfortable with your chosen planner, it's also important to make sure that you're developing the right kind of relationship. These questions should help keep you on track.

Does it feel like they are committed for the long haul? Does it feel like your planner is ready to engage in a generational relationship with your family? The maximum duration of a trust is 125 years - your planner should be prepared to think on this scale.

Does their approach feel flexible, and suited to your situation? Some clients prefer to take things step-by-step, whilst others need everything to be taken care of all in one go. Your planner should be responsive to your particular needs.

Does your planner challenge you on important decisions? Whilst they're ultimately there to help you deliver your vision, it's vital that your planner can tell you if they think you're making a mistake. After all, "Yes Men" usually make poor advisors.

Standard of service

As well as the "soft" elements of the estate planning relationship, there are also certain best practice standards that you should look out for. These include:

Do they charge a fixed rate? A good estate planner will always be upfront with their costs, and never try to lure clients in with teaser rates that shoot up once you're on the hook.

Do they uncover sources of wealth and/or liabilities that you would never have thought to look for? A good estate planner should be working to add value to your estate at every opportunity.

Are they your single point of contact for all your estate planning needs, providing access to third-party expertise where required? Your planner should never be telling you to figure things out for yourself, or to find help on your own.

Is their plan future-proof? Everything your estate planner does should be clearly and properly documented so that the work can be handed over to and continued by another professional or even a different legal firm. This means that if your planner retires or their firm closes down, all your plans will still be valid. At Sure Wealth, we guarantee that all our documentation is transferable to any other reputable practitioner in the UK.

To cut a long story short, an estate planner should not just be someone who supplies you with a service, but a trusted family advisor. Speaking for myself, this is the part of the job I've always really loved.

Meeting new people, getting to know what makes them tick, forging long-lasting relationships, helping clients achieve their ambitions, watching them savour their newfound peace of mind – these are the experiences that motivated me to take up estate planning in the first place. I take deep satisfaction in knowing that the more

I enjoy these experiences, the better the service I'm providing to my clients.

Questions for your estate planner

As we've seen, there's a lot to consider when choosing your estate planner. When it comes down to it, however, you might have to make your decision on the basis of a single meeting or a few short conversations. In cases like these, you need to be able to cut to the chase. Here are six key questions you can use to help discover if the person you're talking to has the necessary skills and qualifications.

1. Are you a member of STEP?
2. Are you affiliated with any other professional bodies?
3. Do you operate on a fixed-fee basis?
4. Are you a generalist or a specialist?
5. Do you use the solutions you recommend yourself?
6. Do I like them as a person?

Conclusion

"All good men and women must take responsibility
to create legacies that will take the next generation
to a level we could only imagine."

--Jim Rohn

Now that we've reached the end of this book, I'd like you to think back to how you felt when you first opened it. Nervous? Confused? Stressed out? Of course, it's impossible to completely remove pain or sadness from the experience of death, but I hope that by hearing my perspective some of these negative feelings might have been reduced, or even replaced by different sensations – confidence, pride, or peace of mind.

We've been through a lot together throughout the preceding chapters. We've learned to face our own mortality with a positive mindset, and begun the process of envisioning our personal legacies. We've understood the importance of planning, and discovered how wealthy we really are. We've seen some of the risks involved with passing on your wealth, and learned how estate planning can mitigate them. We've clarified the benefits of engaging a qualified estate planner, and helped you decide which kind of professional is right for you.

I hope you'll keep this book around, and return to it whenever you need to refresh or refocus. The visions you've sketched and the plans you've made should be revisited regularly, both so you can remind yourself of your goals and so they can be adjusted to fit any changes that take place as time goes by. Your estate plan is a living document, not a gravestone.

If I have one final takeaway to leave you with, it's this:

Dream to live to 100,

but plan like you're going to die tomorrow

If you feel like you're ready to start discussing your plans with a professional, then there's no time like the present. Remember, death waits for no one!

To get in touch about how you can start creating an estate plan that provides financial security and a legacy for your family, feel free to book a wealth planning consultation with me using the QR code below:

About the Author

Ravi Solanki is an Estate Planner and owner of Sure Wealth. He graduated in 2006 from Jesus College, University of Cambridge and holds several estate planning qualifications. He is a member of the Society of Will Writers and a Member of the Society of Trust and Estate Practitioners (STEP).

After graduation, Ravi worked for eleven years in various corporate roles within the banking and finance sectors in London. He thoroughly enjoyed his time here, a nonstop challenge which taught him many invaluable skills and allowed him to meet hundreds of inspiring people. However, he always felt like something vital was missing from his professional life.

In 2017, Ravi left the corporate world behind to join Sure Wealth alongside his brother Kamal. Here, he was able to connect with his true inner calling – helping families achieve financial security and peace of mind. In this new role, Ravi found he could connect with his clients on a much more personal level, learning about their values and ambitions and using this understanding to help them realise their legacy vision. His focus is always to make the often challenging business of estate planning as simple and fulfilling as possible.

When not at work, Ravi enjoys reading, travelling, wine tasting, playing the piano and supporting Arsenal!. He is also the host of The Legacy Show, a podcast which explores estate planning through the prisms of Purpose, Contribution and Legacy – three core concepts which,

Ravi has discovered, motivate people to build wealth for future generations. In each episode, Ravi and a range of experts explore a fresh perspective on the practical, financial, emotional and spiritual dynamics that feed into estate planning. If you've ever found yourself wondering about what kind of legacy you'll leave behind for your loved ones, then tune in weekly for empowering, thought-provoking discussions and debates.

Work with me

You don't have to have it all figured out – that's what I'm here for!

Estate planning doesn't have to be complicated or stressful. And you most certainly don't have to have it all figured out to get started.

All you need to do is book one of my private and confidential Wealth Planning Consultations. I'll help you figure out your priorities and create a plan of action.

During the consultation, we'll discuss:

• Your family

• Your current assets

• Your wishes and ideal outcomes

• Any dangers and risks

• Any specific issues in your family that need
  to be covered

And by the end of the consultation, we will have:

- Mapped out a clear blueprint for your personal legacy
- Built a picture of your existing wealth and created a strategy for how to pass it on
- Identified any risks involved with passing on your wealth and how to mitigate them

After our consultation, you'll receive a detailed action plan on what steps you need to take to get everything in place.

So, if you want a secure future for you and those close to you, book your consultation using the QR code below:

Get your estate planning score today

Estate planning is an investment in the future of your family and their financial security. By taking the time to plan now, you can ensure that your legacy will be protected and your loved ones will be provided for in the years to come.

That's why I've created a scorecard so that you can instantly see where the gaps in your current estate planning are and the action you need to take to ensure you and your family are fully covered.

Quick and Easy to complete

This scorecard will take you less than a minute to complete and is absolutely free.

Instant Results

Answer 12 questions and instantly receive results showing how prepared you are for protecting your wealth.

Targeted insights

You'll receive a personalised insight report with unique feedback tailored to your results.

Find out your score today using the QR code below:

Printed in Great Britain
by Amazon

29719704R00099